W9-BWI-096

A Rookie reader®

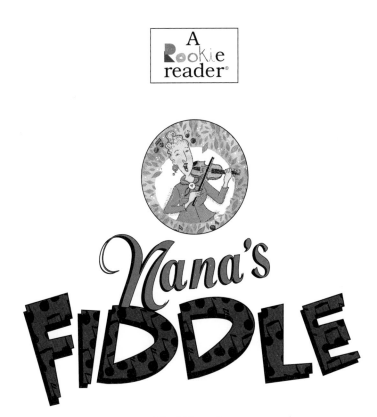

Nana's FIDDLE

Written by
Larry Dane Brimner

Illustrated by
Susan Miller

Children's Press®
A Division of Scholastic Inc.
New York • Toronto • London • Auckland • Sydney
Mexico City • New Delhi • Hong Kong
Danbury, Connecticut

For kids everywhere who have a song to share
—L.D.B.

For Leonard
—S.M.

Reading Consultants

Linda Cornwell
Literacy Specialist

Katharine A. Kane
Education Consultant
(Retired, San Diego County Office of Education
and San Diego State University)

Library of Congress Cataloging-in-Publication Data

Brimner, Larry Dane.
    Nana's fiddle / written by Larry Dane Brimner ; illustrated by Susan Miller.
        p. cm. — (Rookie reader)
    Summary: Although her neighbors are reluctant to listen to her play the fiddle, Nana
persists and her hog steals the show.
    ISBN 0-516-22373-9 (lib. bdg.)   0-516-27820-7 (pbk.)
    [1. Grandmothers—Fiction. 2. Fiddling—Fiction. 3. Pigs—Fiction. 4. Stories in rhyme.]
I. Miller, Susan, 1956- ill. II. Title. III. Series.
PZ8.3.B77145 Nal 2002
[E]—dc21   2001008492

When my nana plays a song,
neighbors stop.

Then they shout,
"That song is far too long."

Do they hear the sound I hear—
a sound that's loud and strong?

They shake their fists.
They plug their ears.

9

Someone groans, "Oh, dear!"

But Nana laughs
and throws a kiss.

14

She gets her fiddle ready.

She lifts her bow
and hollers out,
"Gather around for a
show you shouldn't miss."

They nod and say, "We have to run."

19

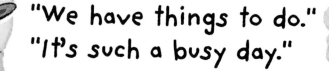

"We have things to do."
"It's such a busy day."

20

22

My nana winks and says to me,
"Shucks! They don't know what's fun."

23

Then Nana tap tap taps her toe and counts out the beat.

She plays fiddle.
I play drum.

And Nana's hog?

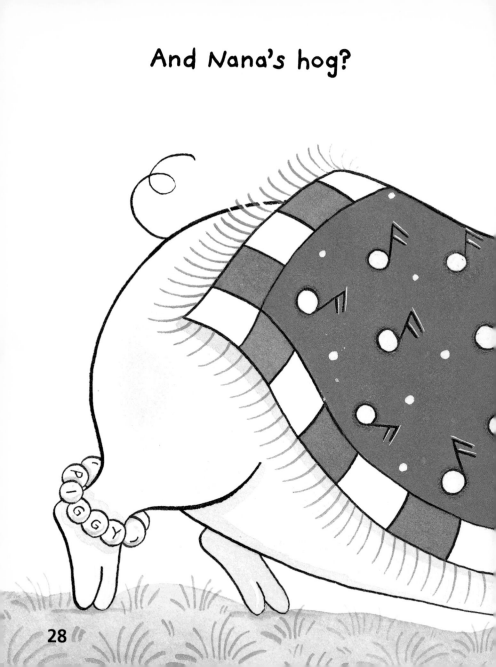

He steals the show.

Word List (84 words)

a	groans	neighbors	stop
and	have	nod	strong
around	he	oh	such
beat	hear	out	tap
bow	her	play	taps
busy	hog	plays	that
but	hollers	plug	that's
counts	I	ready	the
day	is	run	their
dear	it's	say	then
do	kiss	says	they
don't	know	shake	things
drum	laughs	she	throws
ears	lifts	shouldn't	to
far	long	shout	toe
fiddle	loud	show	too
fists	me	shucks	we
for	miss	someone	what's
fun	my	song	when
gather	nana	sound	winks
gets	Nana's	steals	you

About the Author

Larry Dane Brimner has written dozens of fiction and nonfiction books for children on a wide variety of topics. Among his many honors is the 2000 "Celebrate Literacy" award given by the International Reading Association.

About the Illustrator

Susan Miller has illustrated many books for children, including *Nana's Hog* in the Rookie Reader series. She is especially happy to see Nana return, playing her fiddle. When she is not illustrating, she enjoys making crafts and spending time with friends and family. She lives in the rural Litchfield Hills of Connecticut.